**Bibliographic information published by the German National Library:**

The German National Library lists this publication in the National Bibliography; detailed bibliographic data are available on the Internet at http://dnb.dnb.de .

**Imprint:**

Copyright © 2018 GRIN Verlag
Print and binding: Books on Demand GmbH, Norderstedt Germany
ISBN: 9783346053978

**This book at GRIN:**

https://www.grin.com/document/506614

Difrine Madara

# Risk Management Strategies and the Role of Senior Managers

GRIN Verlag

**GRIN - Your knowledge has value**

Since its foundation in 1998, GRIN has specialized in publishing academic texts by students, college teachers and other academics as e-book and printed book. The website www.grin.com is an ideal platform for presenting term papers, final papers, scientific essays, dissertations and specialist books.

**Visit us on the internet:**

http://www.grin.com/

http://www.facebook.com/grincom

http://www.twitter.com/grin_com

## Contents

## INTRODUCTION

Risks are inevitable in any business organisation. In this case, a company must put in place comprehensive measures to address various types of risks that a company may face. A senior manager of any organisation has a significant role to play in designing risk management strategy for the company. This report is, therefore, about the role of senior management in risk assessment, development of the company's risk management strategy, communication and resourcing risk management strategies and the evaluation of outcomes.

# TASK 1

A.C. 1.1

Risk management can be defined as the process of identifying, evaluating and prioritising risks supported by a well-coordinated efficient investment of resources to minimise, monitor and control the probability of the occurrence of the unfortunate events and maximise attainment of opportunities (Al-Thani & Merna, 2013). Risks originate from several sources, such as uncertainty in the financial markets, threats of project failure, legal issues, accidents, credit risks, and natural occurrences, among others. There are also cases where some events that have never happened before can occur, such as 9/11 terror attacks. These risks are referred to as 'unforeseeable risks'. According to NassimTaleb, unforeseeable risks are events, which are the rare but high impact on the business or organisation (Lambert, 2010). In the contemporary business environment, inventions, such as social media and natural issues, such as global warming can have a massive impact on business thus the management should prepare for such issues or events appropriately.

Risk management, therefore, encompasses strategies adopted by the organisation to ensure that the negative effects of these uncertainties are limited by avoiding, reducing, transferring or accepting the risk. However, risk management initiatives must also consider strategic risks. Basically, strategic risks refer to long-term risks that may arise from long-term decisions taken by the company. That is, a strategic risk refers to potential losses that the company may incur as a result of pursuing wrong business or long-term plans (Al-Thani & Merna, 2013). In this regard, strategic risk management could be described as identifying, assessing and managing risks process that arises from the company's business strategy, which includes taking necessary actions if such risks are identified. It encompasses the evaluation of a broad range of probable incidents and circumstances that may disturb the company's strategy and its performance.

A.C. 1.2

Senior management includes senior executives with significant responsibilities for risk management in the company. They include chief risk officer, chief financial officer, chief legal officer, and chief audit executive, just to name a few. The main role of senior management in risk management is to offer support to the organisation's risk management philosophy and vision, ensure compliance with its risk appetite and oversee management of risks in a manner consistent with their respective risk tolerances (Lambert, 2010).

The senior management influences the company's attitude toward risk. For instance, when the company is willing to take higher risks, then the potential returns should also be equally high. On the other hand, low-risk investments are likely to offer lower returns to the company (Hubbard, 2009). A good attitude to risk implies that the chosen investments are well balanced and the available money and assets can help the company realise its objectives within a particular timeframe. There are at least four different criteria that can be used by the management in making decisions regarding uncertainties. For example, Hurwicz — optimism–pessimism criterion focuses on finding a middle ground between risk and opportunity by choosing an outcome, which has the best combination of pay-off and loss while Wald - maximin criterion attempts to select an alternative that is least risky regardless of the opportunity. Other criteria include Savage — minimax or regret criterion, which considers the maximum opportunity value and Laplace — insufficient reason criterion, which is in cases where there is lack of information on the likelihood of various outcomes (Lambert, 2010). In this scenario, the criterion assumes all likelihoods are equal thus the alternative with the highest average opportunity value is selected.

In the meantime, Allan and Beer experiment on risk vulnerability of managers found that manager's risk awareness was inversely proportional to the actual exposure to risk (Lambert, 2010). That is, the more aware the managers were of risks and its interdependencies in specific areas, the less likely these risks would occur in that area. The findings of this experiment implied that by awareness of risks by the senior managers was a crucial step in risk management thus organisations should always invest in identification and measuring of its risk perception. In addition, the senior management plays a role of risk oversight through development of policies and procedures, which are in harmony with the company's strategy & risk appetite and follow up management's implementation of risk management policies and procedures, taking steps to foster risk awareness, and encouraging an organisation culture of risk adjusting awareness (Al-Thani & Merna, 2013).

In line with the risk management roles of senior management highlighted in the text, they have a responsibility to oversee, evaluate and monitor risk management strategy of the organisation. First, the senior management must acknowledge that every activity within an organisation comprises of some degree of threat or uncertainty. The management must ensure that both generic and inherent threats are identified to limit the risk of failure of a particular activity. Second, the senior management has a responsibility to evaluate the probability of occurrence of such risks and estimate the possible impact and cost of the risk on the project. Finally, the management must design and implement a strategy to assist in the management of the prioritised risks (Al-Thani & Merna, 2013). The management develops a plan that outlines various steps to be undertaken in the management of major risks while also allowing the project to continue with minimal probability of failure. Some of the strategies that can be adopted include avoidance strategy, modification strategy, retention strategy and sharing strategy (Al-Thani & Merna, 2013). Avoidance strategy encompasses the development of an action plan that focuses on the complete cessation of service provision or project. Modification strategy aims at changing project tasks to reduce the possibility of the threat occurring. Retention strategy refers to management acknowledging the risks thus preparing for the consequences by first accepting them. Lastly, the management can adopt a risk-sharing strategy, which refers to signing an agreement with a third party to share costs, such as insurance.

A.C. 1.3

Recent studies indicated that there are several examples of qualitative and quantitative risk models. Some of the most common examples include enterprise risk management model (ERM), ISO 31000:2009, MoR (Management of Risk) framework among others (Lambert, 2010). ERM is a standardised framework used to develop, revise and review the objectives of the company vis-à-vis the risks that it may be exposed to. ERM model is effective for risk management as it allows for risks and costs to be evaluated comprehensively. It also allows for the identification of mechanisms that can be used to address constraints and take advantage of opportunities (Hubbard, 2009). The model also allows the company to focus its resources on the management of the downside of risks as well as the upside they represent. Therefore, the model will help organisation leaders to develop a strategic plan to address risks thus enhancing investor confidence in the company. Despite its numerous advantages, the model has two main disadvantages that may hinder its effective implementation. First, employing ERM is costly and takes a lot of time. Second, if the risks and opportunities are not well understood, the model could lead to incorrect strategies being implemented. Nevertheless, if the model is used in a systematic and disciplined manner, its benefits will outweigh weaknesses by a huge margin.

Another important example of a risk management model is the ISO 31000:2009. The main purpose of ISO 31000:2009 is to provide principles and generic guidelines on risk management. The main advantage of this model is that its guidelines and principles can be applied throughout the life of the company thus it helps in decision making regarding operations,

5

service delivery and even core assets. The model also facilitates standardisation of risk management plans and strategies throughout the company. Due to its simplicity, the model has been accepted by many at the workplace. Nevertheless, concern remains regarding what happens after the outcomes of the risk assessment process have been found. Despite this limitation, this model is more effective as it makes the scheme's execution of risk management plans and framework under this model rely on the unique needs of the specific company, specific goals, structure, context, functions, assets and specific practices much simpler (Hubbard, 2009).

## TASK 2

### A.C. 2.1

On the other hand, ISO 31000:2009 risk criteria is designed to empower strategic, management and operational tasks of a company across various projects, functions and processes are lined up to a common set of risk management objectives (Hubbard, 2009). This criterion is the most effective as it provides a clear framework for risk management regardless of the organisation's size, activity and sector. The criteria can also help organisations to enhance the likelihood of achieving objectives, improve the identification of opportunities and threats and effectively allocate and use resources for risk treatment (Lambert, 2010).

This appropriateness of this approach is also based on its ability to help in classifying risks based on their effect and frequency in accordance with the scales used within the organisation. Basic risk management criteria should be as shown in table 1 (not included in this publication).

Based on the criteria, specific risks are then evaluated in terms of frequency, i.e. frequent, likely, occasional, seldom and unlikely. The risk criteria should then be combined with occurrence frequency leading to a consistent risk classification scheme consisting of extremely high risk (E), high risk (H), moderate risk (M) and low risk (L). When the particular risk is extremely high, then the project is at a high chance of failure, thus the management should not implement it. When the risks are high, then there is a high chance of considerable failure in some parts of the project thus the management should consider changing those activities, outsourcing or insurance (Lambert, 2010). When the risks are moderately high, there will be a high chance of noticeable failure in some parts of the project thus insurance will limit the company's exposure. Finally, the management should accept low risks.

A.C. 2.2

There are several techniques that can be used to identify and quantify risks. First, risks can be identified during the information gathering stage; that is, the manager can identify risks facing the company by interviewing other stakeholders, such as for the employees, customers, or even competitors. Risks can also be identified when reviewing project related documents, such as project report, articles, and process assets. Brainstorming with other people can also lead to the identification of risks, which may face the project. For instance, the project manager can consult a team of experts anonymously to obtain the required information. Conducting SWOT, root cause and checklist analysis can also lead to the identification of risks (Al-Thani & Merna, 2013). Second, the development of risk register helps in the ranking of risks that the company project may face. A risk register can be defined as an updated document throughout the life cycle of the project and include historical records, which can be used for future projects. Some of the main components of the risk register include a list of risks, a list of potential responses, root causes of risks, and updated risk categories.

The manager can use techniques, such as probability and impact matrix and risk data quality assessment to quantify risks identified using qualitative models highlighted above. Probability and impact matrix assist in the identification of risks that require an immediate response from the company. The matrix is usually designed depending on project needs. However, some organisations have standardised templates for probability and impact matrix which are used by managers to leverage risks, which are repeatable within the project. On the other hand, risk data quality assessment is used where data is collated for the identified risks. The project manager uses this approach in an attempt to find data accuracy, which has to be analysed to complete the qualitative analysis of risks. In Risk Data Quality Assessment, the project manager has to determine the extent of the understanding of the risk, the existing data, quality and consistency and integrity of the data for each risk (Lambert, 2010).

It is important to note that in some cases; the risks identified may be co-occurring or interdependent. In the context of ERM, risk interdependencies must never be ignored in identification and quantification of risks. To ensure proper risk management within an organisation, a variety of risks must be understood alongside their dependency characteristics. That is, most of the ERM practices rely on the understanding of interdependence, especially in regard to risk measurement and risk capital determination (Lambert, 2010). In this regard, the best risk management strategy should encompass spreading risk exposures among less interdependent strategic choices where the organisation have the skills and experience to perform well while giving a careful consideration that interdependence often requires measurement.

TASK 3

A.C 2.3

Risk mitigation strategies refer to the different ways used by managers to deal with risks in their companies. However, before a mitigation strategy is developed, the company must assess the risk to ensure that the existing controls are sufficient and if the risks are acceptable for the organisation. According to ISO Guide 73:2009, risk evaluation encompasses a comparison of the results of risk analysis against risk criteria to determine whether risks and their magnitude is acceptable or tolerable (Lambert, 2010). The results of risk evaluation will guide the manager in determining an appropriate risk mitigation strategy to adopt i.e. risk avoidance, risk transfer, elimination, sharing, and reduction to an acceptable level. Notably, in most cases, the company will not be able to eliminate risk, thus they will have to accept, avoid or minimise their exposure to the adverse effects of such risks. Risk acceptance refers to the decision not to take any action to reduce the risk thus accepting its possible consequences. Risk reduction strategy implies taking measures to reduce the overall impact of the risk to an acceptable level. Risk transfer, on the other hand, refers to transferring the risk to another person or entity. For instance, the company can get the insurance or transfer the risk through outsourcing (Lloyds, 2017). Lastly, risk avoidance strategy is the decision not to go ahead with the intention due to the risk; that is, the company may decide not to launch the product or conclude the contract.

In most cases, mitigation strategies, such as risk acceptance and avoidance, may not be economically feasible. Furthermore, some strategies may require a vast amount of resources so as to be successful. In these cases, the most viable risk mitigation strategy should minimise the risk level as low as reasonably practicable. The strategy should be balanced with measures to reduce some risks and eliminate others (Lloyds, 2017). For example, there are various aspects of costs, time, and complexities associated with a project that can be minimised or eliminated and still be able to attain the best possible outcomes. For instance, some labour costs can be eliminated by avoiding job duplication or by employing technology. The best mitigation strategy should also reduce the risk probability, the severity of its outcome as well as the overall organisation's exposure to risk.

For optimal results, which is a combination of mitigation strategies, can be employed. For example, the manager should avoid investments that lead to the high probability of financial losses and damages and transfer those projects where there is a low probability of risks taking but the risks could have huge financial implications to the company if left. The company should accept risks where mitigation expenses are more than the cost of tolerating the risks. In such cases, the manager should carefully monitor the mitigation expenses (Spina, 2013). Finally,

9

risk limitation involves taking some action to address the perceived risk and regulate company exposure. Risk limitation involves adopting both risk acceptance and avoidance measures.

Specifically, a production facility or organisation can implement the risk strategies identified in the text as shown in table 2.

Table 2: Risk strategies

| Strategy | Action plan |
|---|---|
| Avoidance | Use a standard machine or equipment part to produce the product or outsource the product from another company |
| Transfer | Use insurance to mitigate warranty costs |
| Mitigation | Inspect all parts of the plant quality levels and reduce the breakdown rates with regular maintenance |
| Acceptance | Take the chance that no problem will arise and continue with production |

A.C. 2.4

Good communication is necessary for effective planning and implementation of the risk management strategy. Effective risk management involves all the company's stakeholders, such as the board of directors, and members of staff, among others (Lloyds, 2017). It is, therefore, important that everybody understand what the risk management entails and why it is important for the company. Communication must therefore be a core component of risk management process. The information that the management shares vary depending on the audience, however, it has to make should that all stakeholders are involved throughout the risk management cycle. That is, an effective communication strategy should be a two-way approach both upwards and downwards (Lambert, 2010). The objective of the communication should include building and maintaining trust among all stakeholders, ensuring that the language used is appropriate for all audience, being clear and transparent and respecting the opinions of other stakeholders.

To build trust and maintain trust, the management should also ensure consistency of information but not at the expense of accuracy. In the case where the information is inconsistent with what other stakeholders know from the past, the management must acknowledge changes or previous mistakes and then explain the situation as it stands (Al-Thani & Merna, 2013). In addition, the risk management communication strategy should consider who the audience are and ensure that the language and type of communication is tailored for them. In addition, the management should make sure that the information is conveyed in a way that leads to your organization's desired actions and outcomes in a manner that is clear and transparent for the targeted audience. By being clear, the communication should be in a direct, simple and understandable manner. For instance, there should be no use of jargon in discussion of situation. On the other hand, transparency means that the risk management team must disclose assumptions, methodologies, and uncertainties (Al-Thani & Merna, 2013). Finally, it is important for the risk communicator to answer questions and provide options. To enhance integrity of the information, the communicated message should encompass acknowledgement of uncertainties, recognize limitations, debate assumptions and distinguish between results that are and are not supported by analysis.

## TASK 4

A.C. 3.1

The expectation of every organisation is to ensure that the risk mitigation strategies adopted are effective in minimising the probability of risk occurrence and the overall impact of risks on the company and its activities. GRC capability model allows for the development of a more sustainable organisational hierarchy. That is, embedding organisational hierarchy in a GRC tool is a task that is often overlooked but can have tremendous value for all the departments in the organisation, including Audit, Compliance/Risk/Vendor Management, and Information Security, among others. The model also creates a "one-stop shop" for GRC process results for functions, such as audit, risk assessment, regulation compliance, and assessing suppliers. The model also ensures process consolidation and greater consistency. For instance, GRC tool workflow capabilities and configuration flexibility make it possible to centralise and improve the consistency of organisation GRC processes.

On the negative side, the task of measuring the potential benefits of risk management to an organisation is a challenging one using this model. However, to overcome this challenge, measuring risk management performance will be assessed based on factors, such as compliance, maturity, and value addition. An effective GRC capability framework ensures that there is a consistent evidence-based decision-making approach at all levels of the organisation, i.e. organisation resources will be spent in a more efficient manner. The risk management framework should also ensure that the change activities implemented within the company have a better chance of succeeding.

The framework also ensures that the company is able to anticipate and capitalise on the external changes within the business environment. Some of these external changes include demographic changes, customers' expectations, and government policy. An effective risk management framework should also ensure that all employees focus and prioritise actions that can help the company to execute strategies and project plans, which are consistent with its strategic objectives (Lloyds, 2017). The framework also ensures accountability for risks and most significantly, put in place controls and monitoring initiatives for the project. With time, the effective risk management strategy will lead to considerable changes on the organisation culture as the companies' employees will be engaging in activities, which directly impact on the attainment of the organisational goals and objectives thus ensuring successful completion of projects.

A.C. 3.2

Traditionally, companies invested in structured risk management programs, which were based on the regulatory requirements and management priorities. However, contemporary risk management programs emphasise the additional pressures, such as protection of the market value, stakeholder expectations and associated risks, and the need for the management to demonstrate reasonable risk awareness (Spina, 2013). Some of the actions of the company that will ensure that positive risk management outcomes highlighted in Task 4 (a) are realised include the development of risk culture, determining risk appetite, precisely identifying the risks, performing risk assessment, and risk monitoring, among others. A good risk culture offer support to risk management initiatives and incorporates risk management into executive communications and facilitates the establishment of appropriate risk management behaviours (Spina, 2013). The company can develop a code of conduct that incorporates performance evaluation plans, role definition and motivation strategies. In addition, determining the organisation's risk appetite helps the staff to understand specific risks, which the organisation is willing to take thus ensuring that the management and board have the opportunity to align the views on risk before the incident occurs.

In the meantime, the organisation's risk identification processes must start from planning. At the planning stage, the organisation should evaluate all layers of management and their alignment to the business processes and strategies. Some of the risks that can be identified by evaluating the plan include operational, legal, and reputational risks. The manager also suggests that risks be identified using other methods, such as interviews, surveys, and facilitated workshops (Greuning & Brajovic, 2009). Besides, the company should perform a risk assessment that clarifies risk objectives. As part of the risk assessment process, the manager must first clearly define issues related to risks, such as inherent versus residual risk, risk levels and the adequacy of controls, should be clearly communicated. For example, the manager must recognise that risk with high probability results in losses on a daily basis while a risk with high impact would result in considerable harm to the company's reputation. Risk monitoring should be conducted after risk assessments. Lastly, an emphasis on risk reporting helps to highlight key risks and recommendations for management action.

Table 3, therefore, highlights some of the responses outcomes of risk management criteria and possible action plan.

Table 3: Risk management outcomes

| Risk type | Event | Action | Plan |
|---|---|---|---|
| Compli-ance risks | Failure to meet compliance ob-ligations | Avoid | ✓ Identify compliance requirements<br>✓ Identify appropriate system or tools to manage compliance requirements<br>✓ Conduct monthly reviews to ensure no compliance breaches |
| Legal risks | Loss of a practi-tioner | Reduce | ✓ Appoint an attorney<br>✓ Document key processes<br>✓ Put in place client management system for adequate documentation<br>✓ Train secondary level management |
| Sales risks | Failure to col-lect receivables in a timely man-ner | Reduce | ✓ Identify requirements to track receivables<br>✓ Develop procedures of tracking aged debtors and receivables<br>✓ Consider monitoring requirements including frequency |

# TASK 5

A.C. 3.3

This is a disaster recovery plan for a fire emergency in a banking hall

## General Overview

The aim of the bank is to ensure continuous business for all its functions or activities within its banking hall. To do so, the bank must develop a comprehensive disaster policy for all types of hazards that must be adhered to by all employees at the hall. In case of disasters, such as fire breakout, the bank must ensure that employees and all the customers are safe. In addition, the disaster plan should offer effective procedures of safeguarding assets and all the customer accounts.

## Objectives of the Plan

Fire is an uncertain event that can occur within the banking hall at any time due to factors, such as an electrical fault. During fire breakout, several activities at the bank will be negatively impacted, thus the need for employees and sufficient resources to be deployed to ensure quick response to the hazard. In this regard, the plan is designed to provide clear, concise, and essential directions to enhance recovery from different degrees of fire damages within the banking hall.

## Defined Scenario

In this plan, a fire disaster is defined as a disruption of the normal banking functions by the fire where the predictable time for the organisation to return to normal/as usual is uncertain. Fir disasters also refer to fire threats or alarms that lead to the hasty relocation of employees and customers from the hall within a period of time leading to losses and massive interruption of normal activities.

Recovery Objectives

During the fire disaster, the banking intends to realise the following recovery objectives: "

i.   To ensure the safety of all the bank's employees throughout the emergency condition, disaster declaration and recovery processes

ii.  To reestablish all the bank's essential services within the recovery window, i.e. 24 hours

iii. To suspend all non-essential banks' services until normalcy is restored

iv.  To mitigate the impact of the disaster on the customers by rapidly implementing effective recovery strategies

v.   To reduce confusion and misinformation that may be associated with the disaster by availing clear command and control structures

vi.  To consider relocation of personnel and facilities as a recovery strategy of last resort"

Plan Assumptions

This recovery plan was prepared under several assumptions so that the plan can be able to address a wider scope of disasters. Some of the assumptions include:

➢ The recovery efforts are based on the premise that the resources used in recovery initiatives come from outside the affected facility

➢ All the vital documents needed for the recovery can either be retrieved or recreated from outside the affected facility

Business Impact Analysis

The manager should quantify the monetary value of losses of physical assets, work hours and labour among others. The manager should also be able to quantify the monetary value of the inconveniences and disruptions in operations caused by the disaster.

A.C. 3.4

There are several factors that impact the review of the disaster plan like the one illustrated in Task 5 (a). First, disaster plans involve people, such as staff and contractors. During the time of disaster, the company may require people with unique skills that can help in disaster recovery plan implementation, disaster documentation, and knowledge transfer. In some cases, the company may lack people with these skills (Lloyds, 2017). Second, during disasters, the company's physical facilities are in some cases destroyed and there are no alternate areas for people to work from, thus leading to chaos in the implementation of the recovery plan. Lack of alternate site also leads to new challenges, such as site security, staff access procedure, and the need to secure a new facility on a temporary basis (Greuning & Brajovic, 2009). Third, technology also a major factor in disaster plans and reviews. During disasters, technology is important in accessing the equipment space. Some of the technological applications that can facilitate recovery include suitable heating, ventilation, and air conditioning (HVAC) for IT systems, availability of backup systems and the existence of physical and information security capabilities.

Another factor that may impact of disaster plan reviews is data. Some of the areas to look during disasters include securing the storage area, methods of data storage, such as disks, connectivity, and bandwidth requirements, as well as the data protection capabilities of the alternate site. Suppliers of some of the essential tools and materials for recovery are also needed. At this time, the management of the company will have to identify and contract suppliers within a short notice. Finally, the company's policies and procedures in relation to disaster recovery

18

may also impede disaster plan reviews (Greuning & Brajovic, 2009). For instance, the company

policy may require all disaster policies for data recovery to be approved by senior management.

# References

Al-Thani, F. F., &Merna, T. (2013).*Corporate risk management*. Hoboken, NJ: Wiley.

Greuning, H, &Brajovic, B. S. (2009).Analyzing banking risk: A framework for assessing corporate governance and risk management. Washington, DC: World Bank.

Hubbard, D. W. (2009). *The failure of risk management*. Hoboken: John Wiley and Sons.

Lambert, J. (2010).*Developing Risk Management Strategies*. Corby: Chartered Management Institute.

Lloyds. (2017). *Annual Report and Accounts 2017*. Lloyds Banking Group.

Spina, J. J. (2013). Risks in Contemporary Banking Industry.*SSRN Electronic Journal*. doi:10.2139/ssrn.2277772

# YOUR KNOWLEDGE HAS VALUE

- We will publish your bachelor's and
  master's thesis, essays and papers

- Your own eBook and book -
  sold worldwide in all relevant shops

- Earn money with each sale

Upload your text at www.GRIN.com
and publish for free

CPSIA information can be obtained
at www.ICGtesting.com
Printed in the USA
LVHW091943060821
694731LV00017B/1532